Mediterranean Recipes For Breakfast And Brunch

Easy And Delicious Recipes For Breakfast And Brunch In Mediterranean Style

Sommario

Introduction

Breakfast and brunch are the most important meals of the day, and the ancient populations of the Mediterranean knew this well.

They have structured since ancient times tasty recipes, nutritious and full of energy, to be able to face the day, and what is the best way if not to start with the taste?

But let's not lose heart, let's prepare a good coffee and let's start cooking, good morning.

Breakfast & Brunch Recipes

Mediterranean Breakfast Egg White Sandwich

Servings: 1

Cooking Time: 30 Minutes

Ingredients:

- 1 tsp vegan butter

- ¼ cup egg whites

- 1 tsp chopped fresh herbs such as parsley, basil, rosemary

- 1 whole grain seeded ciabatta roll

- 1 tbsp pesto

- 1-2 slices muenster cheese (or other cheese such as provolone, Monterey Jack, etc.)

- About ½ cup roasted tomatoes

- Salt, to taste

- Pepper, to taste

- Roasted Tomatoes:

- 10 oz grape tomatoes

- 1 tbsp extra virgin olive oil

- Kosher salt, to taste

- Coarse black pepper, to taste

Directions:

1. In a small nonstick skillet over medium heat, melt the vegan butter

2. Pour in egg whites, season with salt and pepper, sprinkle with fresh herbs, cook for 3-4 minutes or until egg is done, flip once

3. In the meantime, toast the ciabatta bread in toaster

4. Once done, spread both halves with pesto

5. Place the egg on the bottom half of sandwich roll, folding if necessary, top with cheese, add the roasted tomatoes and top half of roll sandwich

6. To make the roasted tomatoes: Preheat oven to 400 degrees F. Slice tomatoes in half

lengthwise. Then place them onto a baking sheet and drizzle with the olive oil, toss to coat. Season with salt and pepper and roast In oven for about 20 minutes, until the skin appears wrinkled

Nutrition Info:Per Serving: Calories:458;Total Carbohydrates: 51g;Total Fat: 0g;Protein: 21g

Strawberry-apricot Smoothie

Servings: 2

Cooking Time: 15 Minutes

Ingredients:

- 1 cup strawberries, frozen

- ¾ cup almond milk, unsweetened

- 2 apricots, pitted and sliced

Directions:

1. Put all the Ingredients: into the blender.

2. Blend them for a minute or until you reach desired foamy texture.

3. Serve the smoothie.

4. Enjoy.

Nutrition Info:Per Serving: Calories: 247, Total Fat: 21.9 g, Saturated Fat: 19 g, Cholesterol: 0 mg, Sodium: 1mg, Total Carbohydrate: 14.4 g, Dietary Fiber: 4.1 g, Total Sugars: 9.7 g, Protein: 3 g, Vitamin D: 0 mcg, Calcium: 30 mg, Iron: 2 mg, Potassium: 438 mg

Apple Quinoa Breakfast Bars

Servings: 12

Cooking Time: 40 Minutes

Ingredients:

- 2 eggs

- 1 apple peeled and chopped into ½ inch chunks

- 1 cup unsweetened apple sauce

- 1 ½ cups cooked & cooled quinoa

- 1 ½ cups rolled oats

- 1/4 cup peanut butter

- 1 tsp vanilla

- 1/2 tsp cinnamon

- 1/4 cup coconut oil

- ½ tsp baking powder

Directions:

1. Heat oven to 350 degrees F

2. Spray an 8x8 inch baking dish with oil, set aside

3. In a large bowl, stir together the apple sauce, cinnamon, coconut oil, peanut butter, vanilla and eggs

4. Add in the cooked quinoa, rolled oats and baking powder, mix until completely incorporated

5. Fold in the apple chunks

6. Spread the mixture into the prepared baking dish, spreading it to each corner

7. Bake for 40 minutes, or until a toothpick comes out clean

8. Allow to cool before slicing

9. Wrap the bars individually in plastic wrap. Store in an airtight container or baggie in the freezer for up to a month.

10. To serve: Warm up in the oven at 350 F for 5 minutes or microwave for up to 30 seconds

Nutrition Info:Per Serving: (1 bar): Calories:230;Total Fat: 10g;Total Carbs: 31g;Protein: 7g

Pepper, Kale, And Chickpea Shakshuka

Servings: 5

Cooking Time: 35 Minutes

Ingredients:

- 1 tablespoon olive oil

- 1 small red onion, thinly sliced

- 1 red bell pepper, thinly sliced

- 1 green bell pepper, thinly sliced

- 1 bunch kale, stemmed and roughly chopped

- ½ cup packed cilantro leaves, chopped

- ½ teaspoon kosher salt

- 1 teaspoon smoked paprika

- 1 (14.5-ounce) can diced tomatoes

- 1 (14-ounce) can low-sodium chickpeas, drained and rinsed

- ⅔ cup water

- 5 eggs

- 2½ whole-wheat pitas (optional)

Directions:

1. Preheat the oven to 375°F.

2. Heat the oil in an oven-safe 1inch skillet over medium-high heat. Once the oil is shimmering, add the onions and red and green bell peppers. Sauté for 5 minutes, then cover, leaving the lid slightly ajar. Cook for 5 more minutes, then add the kale and cover, leaving the lid slightly ajar. Cook for 10 more minutes, stirring occasionally.

3. Add the cilantro, salt, paprika, tomatoes, chickpeas, and water, and stir to combine.

4. Make 5 wells in the mixture. Break an egg into a small bowl and pour it into a well. Repeat with the remaining eggs.

5. Place the pan in the oven and bake until the egg whites are opaque and the eggs still jiggle a little when the pan is shaken, about 12 to 1minutes, but start checking at 8 minutes.

6. When the shakshuka is cool, scoop about 1¼ cups of veggies into each of 5 containers, along with 1 egg each. If using, place ½ pita in each of 5 resealable bags.

7. STORAGE: Store covered containers in the refrigerator for up to 5 days.

Nutrition Info:Per Serving: Total calories: 244; Total fat: 9g; Saturated fat: 2g; Sodium: 529mg; Carbohydrates: 29g; Fiber: ; Protein: 14g

Rosemary Broccoli Cauliflower Mash

Servings: 3

Cooking Time: 12 Minutes

Ingredients:

- 2 cups broccoli, chopped

- 1 lb cauliflower, cut into florets

- 1 tsp dried rosemary

- 1/4 cup olive oil

- 1 tsp garlic, minced

- Salt

Directions:

1. Add broccoli and cauliflower into the instant pot. Pour enough water into the pot to cover broccoli and cauliflower.

2. Seal pot with lid and cook on high for 1minutes.

3. Once done, allow to release pressure naturally. Remove lid.

4. Drain broccoli and cauliflower well and clean the instant pot.

5. Add oil into the pot and set the pot on sauté mode.

6. Add broccoli, cauliflower, rosemary, garlic, and salt and cook for 10 minutes.

7. Mash the broccoli and cauliflower mixture using a potato masher until smooth.

8. Serve and enjoy.

Nutrition Info: Calories: 205;Fat: 17.2 g;Carbohydrates: 12.6 g;Sugar: 4.7 g;Protein: 4.8 g;Cholesterol: 0 mg

Pumpkin, Apple, And Greek Yogurt Muffins

Servings: 12

Cooking Time: 20 Minutes

Ingredients:

- Cooking spray to grease baking liners

- 2 cups whole-wheat flour

- 1 teaspoon aluminum-free baking powder (see tip)

- 1 teaspoon baking soda

- ⅛ teaspoon kosher salt

- 2 teaspoons ground cinnamon

- ½ teaspoon ground ginger

- ½ teaspoon ground allspice

- ⅔ cup pure maple syrup

- 1 cup low-fat (2%) plain Greek yogurt

- 1 cup 100% canned pumpkin

- 1 large egg

- ¼ cup extra-virgin olive oil

- 1½ cups chopped green apple (leave peel on)

- ½ cup walnut pieces

Directions:

1. Preheat the oven to 400°F and line a muffin tin with baking liners. Spray the liners lightly with cooking spray.

2. In a large bowl, whisk together the flour, baking powder, baking soda, salt, cinnamon, ginger, and allspice.

3. In a medium bowl, combine the maple syrup, yogurt, pumpkin, egg, olive oil, chopped apple, and walnuts.

4. Pour the wet ingredients into the dry ingredients and combine just until blended. Do not overmix.

5. Scoop about ¼ cup of batter into each muffin liner and bake for 20 minutes, or until the tops look browned and a paring knife comes out clean when inserted. Remove the muffins from the tin to cool.

6. STORAGE: Store covered containers at room temperature for up to 4 days. To freeze the

muffins for up to 3 months, wrap them in foil and place in an airtight resealable bag.

Nutrition Info:Per Serving: Total calories: 221; Total fat: 9g; Saturated fat: 1g; Sodium: 18g; Carbohydrates: 32g; Fiber: 4g; Protein: 6g

Cocoa And Raspberry Overnight Oats

Servings: 5

Cooking Time: 10 Minutes

Ingredients:

- 1⅔ cups rolled oats

- 3⅓ cups unsweetened vanilla almond milk

- 2 teaspoons vanilla extract

- 1 tablespoon plus 2 teaspoons pure maple syrup

- 3 tablespoons chia seeds

- 3 tablespoons unsweetened cocoa powder

- 1⅔ cups frozen raspberries

- 5 teaspoons cocoa nibs (optional)

Directions:

1. In a large bowl, mix the oats, almond milk, vanilla, maple syrup, chia seeds, and cocoa powder until well combined.

2. Spoon ¾ cup of the oat mixture into each of 5 containers.

3. Top each serving with ⅓ cup of raspberries and 1 teaspoon of cocoa nibs, if using.

4. STORAGE: Store covered containers in the refrigerator for up to 5 days.

Nutrition Info:Per Serving: Total calories: 21 Total fat: 6g; Saturated fat: <1g; Sodium: 121mg; Carbohydrates: 34g; Fiber: 10g; Protein: 7g

Bacon Brie Omelet With Radish Salad

Servings: 6

Cooking Time: 10 Minutes

Ingredients:

- 200 g smoked lardons

- 3 teaspoons olive oil, divided

- 7 ounces smoked bacon

- 6 lightly beaten eggs

- small bunch chives, snipped up

- 3½ ounces sliced brie

- 1 teaspoon red wine vinegar

- 1 teaspoon Dijon mustard

- 1 cucumber, deseeded, halved, and sliced up diagonally

- 7 ounces radish, quartered

Directions:

1. Heat up the grill.

2. Add 1 teaspoon of oil to a small pan and heat on the grill.

3. Add lardons and fry them until nice and crisp.

4. Drain the lardon on kitchen paper.

5. Heat the remaining 2 teaspoons of oil in a non-sticking pan on the grill.

6. Add lardons, eggs, chives, and ground pepper, and cook over low heat until semi-set.

7. Carefully lay the Brie on top, and grill until it has set and is golden in color.

8. Remove from pan and cut into wedges.

9. Make the salad by mixing olive oil, mustard, vinegar, and seasoning in a bowl.

10. Add cucumber and radish and mix well.

11. Serve the salad alongside the omelet wedges in containers.

12. Enjoy!

Nutrition Info:Per Serving: Calories: 620, Total Fat: 49.3g, Saturated Fat: 22.1, Cholesterol: 295 mg, Sodium: 1632 mg, Total Carbohydrate: 4.3g, Dietary Fiber: 0.9 g, Total Sugars: 2.5 g, Protein: 39.2 g, Vitamin D: 41 mcg, Calcium: 185 mg, Iron: 2 mg, Potassium: 527 mg

Cranberry Oatmeal

Servings: 2

Cooking Time: 6 Minutes

Ingredients:

- 1/2 cup steel-cut oats

- 1 cup unsweetened almond milk

- 1 1/2 tbsp maple syrup

- 1/4 tsp cinnamon

- 1/4 tsp vanilla

- 1/4 cup dried cranberries

- 1 cup of water

- 1 tsp lemon zest, grated

- 1/4 cup orange juice

Directions:

1. Add all ingredients into the heat-safe dish and stir well.

2. Pour 1 cup of water into the instant pot then place the trivet in the pot.

3. Place dish on top of the trivet.

4. Seal pot with lid and cook on high for 6 minutes.

5. Once done, allow to release pressure naturally for 10 minutes then release remaining using quick release. Remove lid.

6. Serve and enjoy.

Nutrition Info: Calories: 161;Fat: 3.2 g;Carbohydrates: 29.9 g;Sugar: 12.4 g;Protein: 3.4 g;Cholesterol: 0 mg

Ricotta Fig Toast

Servings: 1

Cooking Time: 15 Minutes

Ingredients:

- 2 slices whole-wheat toast

- 1 teaspoon honey

- ¼ cup ricotta (partly skimmed)

- 1 dash cinnamon

- 2 figs (sliced)

- 1 teaspoon sesame seeds

Directions:

1. Start by mixing ricotta with honey and dash of cinnamon.

2. Then, spread this mixture on the toast.

3. Now, top with fig and sesame seeds.

4. Serve.

Nutrition Info:Per Serving: Calories: 372, Total Fat: 8.8g, Saturated Fat: 3.8, Cholesterol: 19 mg, Sodium: 373 mg, Total Carbohydrate: .7 g, Dietary Fiber: 8.8 g, Total Sugars: 27.1 g, Protein: 17 g, Vitamin D: 0 mcg, Calcium: 328 mg, Iron: 3 mg, Potassium: 518 mg

Mushroom Goat Cheese Frittata

Servings: 4

Cooking Time: 35 Minutes

Ingredients:

- 1 tbsp olive oil

- 1 small onion, diced

- 10 oz crimini or your favorite mushrooms, sliced

- 1 garlic clove, minced

- 10 eggs

- 2/3 cup half and half

- 1/4 cup fresh chives, minced

- 2 tsp fresh thyme, minced

- 1/2 tsp kosher salt

- 1/2 tsp black pepper

- 4 oz goat cheese

Directions:

1. Preheat the oven to 375 degrees F

2. In an over safe skillet or cast-iron pan over medium heat, olive oil

3. Add in the onion and sauté for 5 mins until golden

4. Add in the sliced mushrooms and garlic, continue to sauté until mushrooms are golden brown, about 10-12 minutes

5. In a large bowl, whisk together the eggs, half and half, chives, thyme, salt and pepper

6. Place the goat cheese over the mushroom mixture and pour the egg mixture over the top

7. Stir the mixture in the pan and cook over medium heat until the edges are set but the center is still loose, about 8-10 minutes

8. Put the pan in the oven and finish cooking for an additional 10 minutes or until set

9. Allow to cool completely before slicing

10. Wrap the slices in plastic wrap and then aluminum foil and place in the freezer.

11. To Serve: Remove the aluminum foil and plastic wrap, and microwave for 2 minutes, then allow to rest for 30 seconds, enjoy!

Nutrition Info:Per Serving: Calories:243;Total Carbohydrates: 5g;Total Fat: 17g;Protein: 15g

Honey, Dried Apricot, And Pistachio Yogurt Parfait

Servings: 3

Cooking Time: 10 Minutes

Ingredients:

- 1 (16-ounce) container low-fat (2%) plain Greek yogurt

- 1 tablespoon honey

- ½ teaspoon rose water (optional)

- ½ cup unsalted shelled pistachios, roughly chopped

- 12 dried apricot halves, quartered

Directions:

1. Mix the yogurt, honey, and rose water (if using) in a medium bowl.

2. Place ⅔ cup of yogurt in each of 3 containers. Top each mound of yogurt with equal portions of the pistachios and apricots.

3. STORAGE: Store covered containers in the refrigerator for up to 7 days.

Nutrition Info:Per Serving: Total calories: 275; Total fat: 12g; Saturated fat: 3g; Sodium: 72mg; Carbohydrates: 26g; Fiber: 3g; Protein: 19g

Mediterranean Stuffed Sweet Potatoes With Chickpeas And Avocado Tahini

Servings: 4

Cooking Time: 40 Minutes

Ingredients:

- 8 medium sized sweet potatoes, rinsed well

- Marinated Chickpeas:

- 1 (15 oz) can chickpeas, drained and rinsed

- 1/2 red pepper, diced

- 3 tbsp extra virgin olive oil

- 1 tbsp fresh lemon juice

- 1 tbsp lemon zest

- 1 clove;about 1/2 teaspoon garlic, crushed

- 1 tbsp freshly chopped parsley

- 1 tbsp fresh oregano

- 1/4 tsp sea salt

- Avocado Tahini Sauce:

- 1 medium sized ripe avocado

- 1/4 cup tahini

- 1/4 cup water

- 1 clove garlic, crushed

- 1 tbsp fresh parsley

- 1 tbsp fresh lemon juice

- Toppings:

- 1/4 cup pepitas, hulled pumpkin seeds

- Crumbled vegan feta or regular feta

Directions:

1. Preheat the oven to 400 degrees F

2. With a fork to pierce a few holes in the sweet potatoes

3. Place them on a baking sheet and bake for 45 minutes to an hour, or until the potatoes are tender to the touch. (Note that larger sweet potato will take longer to bake)

4. In the meantime, prepare the chickpeas by placing them in a medium sized bowl, combine the chickpeas with the extra virgin olive oil, lemon juice, lemon zest, red bell peppers, garlic, parsley, oregano, and sea salt. Toss the

chickpeas until they're all coated in the marinade, set aside

5. Avocado Tahini Sauce:

6. Create the sauce by adding the ripe avocado, tahini, water, garlic, parsley, and lemon juice into a blender and process until smooth - If you would like a thinned consistency add another 1-2 tbsp of water

7. Once smooth transfer the sauce to a small bowl, set aside

8. To Assembly:

9. Once the sweet potatoes are tender, remove them from the oven and set aside until they are cool enough to handle

10. Then cut a slit down the middle of each potato and carefully spoon the chickpeas inside

11. Place the potato and chickpeas bake into container, store for 2-3 days

12. To Serve: Heat through in the oven at 374 degrees F for 5-8 minutes or until heated through. Top with the avocado tahini and sprinkle the pepitas and crumbled feta. Enjoy

13. Recipe Notes: There will be leftover chickpeas & avocado tahini - save the extras to make more sweet potatoes or create a big salad for a different lunch

Nutrition Info:Per Serving: Calories:308;Carbs: 38g;Total Fat: 15g;Protein: 7g

Walnut Banana Oatmeal

Servings: 2

Cooking Time: 3 Minutes

Ingredients:

- 1/2 cup steel-cut oats

- 1 cup of water

- 1 cup unsweetened almond milk

- 1 tsp honey

- 2 tbsp walnuts, chopped

- 1/2 banana, chopped

Directions:

1. Spray instant pot from inside with cooking spray.

2. Add oats, water, and almond milk into the instant pot and stir well.

3. Seal pot with lid and cook on high for minutes.

4. Once done, release pressure using quick release. Remove lid.

5. Stir in honey, walnut, and banana and serve.

Nutrition Info: Calories: 183;Fat: 7.8 g;Carbohydrates: 25.2 g;Sugar: 8 g;Protein: 5.4 g;Cholesterol: 0 mg

Super-seed Granola

Servings: 8

Cooking Time: 40 Minutes

Ingredients:

- 1½ cups rolled oats

- ⅓ cup raw quinoa

- ⅓ cup green pumpkin seeds (pepitas)

- ⅓ cup raw, unsalted sunflower seeds

- 2 tablespoons chia seeds

- 1 teaspoon ground cinnamon

- ⅓ cup pure maple syrup

- ⅓ cup unsweetened, unsalted sunflower seed butter

Directions:

1. Preheat the oven to 325°F. Line a baking sheet with a silicone mat or parchment paper.

2. In a large mixing bowl, combine the oats, quinoa, pumpkin seeds, sunflower seeds, chia seeds, and cinnamon.

3. Place the maple syrup and sunflower seed butter in a small microwaveable bowl and microwave for 20 to seconds to melt the seed butter. Pour it over the oat mixture and stir to coat.

4. Spread the granola evenly across the lined pan, bake for 15 minutes, stir, bake for 15 more minutes, stir, and bake for 10 more minutes. Remove the granola from the oven; it will get crunchier as it cools.

5. Place ½ cup of granola in each of 8 containers and store at room temperature.

6. STORAGE: Store covered containers at room temperature for 2 weeks.

Nutrition Info:Per Serving: Total calories: 258; Total fat: 13g; Saturated fat: 1g; Sodium: 19mg; Carbohydrates: 30g; Fiber: 4g; Protein: 9g

Ham And Egg Muffins

Servings: 6

Cooking Time: 25 Minutes

Ingredients:

- ¼ cup crumbled feta cheese

- ⅛ teaspoon salt

- 1 ½ tablespoons of pesto sauce

- 9 slices of deli ham

- ⅓ cup chopped spinach

- 5 eggs

- ⅛ teaspoon of pepper

- ½ cup roasted red pepper plus a little for garnish

- Basil for garnish

Directions:

1. Turn the temperature on your oven to 400 degrees Fahrenheit.

2. Grease the cups of the muffin tin.

3. Line each muffin tin cup with a slice of ham. The trick is to ensure there are no holes within the ham so none of the egg mixture seeps out.

4. Add some roasted peppers into the muffin cup.

5. Add 1 tablespoon of chopped spinach on top of the roasted pepper.

6. Sprinkle ½ tablespoon of feta cheese on top of the spinach.

7. Combine the eggs in a bowl with the salt and pepper. Whisk well.

8. Divide the egg mixture evenly between the 6 muffin tins.

9. Set in your oven and turn the timer for 15 minutes. If the eggs are not set and puffy after 15 minutes, keep them in the oven for another minute or two.

10. Carefully remove the muffins from the muffin tin cups and let them cool completely.

11. Garnish and enjoy your breakfast muffins, or you can store them in the fridge for up to three days. To warm them up, microwave them for 30 seconds.

Nutrition Info: calories: 109, fats: 6 grams, carbohydrates: 2 grams, protein: 9 grams.

Almond Pancakes

Servings: 6

Cooking Time: 30 Minutes

Ingredients:

- ½ cup melted coconut oil, plus a little on the side for grease

- 2 cups unsweetened, room temperature almond milk

- 2 teaspoons raw honey

- 1 ½ cups whole wheat flour

- 2 eggs, room temperature

- ¼ teaspoon ground cinnamon

- ½ cup almond flour

- ¼ teaspoon sea salt

- ½ teaspoon baking soda

- 1 ½ teaspoons baking powder

Directions:

1. In a large bowl, whisk your eggs.

2. Add in the coconut oil, honey, and almond milk. Whisk thoroughly.

3. In a separate bowl, sift together your baking soda, baking powder, sea salt, almond flour, cinnamon, and whole wheat flour. Ensure the ingredients are well incorporated.

4. Combine the two mixtures by slowly adding your powdered ingredients into your wet ingredients. Stir as you combine as it will be easier to fully mix the ingredients.

5. Grease a large skillet with oil and set it on medium-high heat.

6. Using ½ cup measurements, pour the batter into the skillet. Make sure the pancakes are not touching each other when they cook.

7. Let your pancakes cook for about 3 to 5 minutes on each side. Once bubbles start to break the surface and the edges become firm, flip the pancake over to cook the other side.

8. Once they are cooked thoroughly, place them on a plate and continue the process until all your batter is used up. You might need to grease your skillet again between batches.

9. To give your pancakes more of a Mediterranean flavor, add some fresh fruit on top.

Nutrition Info: calories: 286, fats: 17 grams, carbohydrates: 26 grams, protein: 7 grams.

Mediterranean Egg Muffins With Ham

Servings: 6

Cooking Time: 15 Minutes

Ingredients:

- 9 Slices of thin cut deli ham

- 1/2 cup canned roasted red pepper, sliced + additional for garnish

- 1/3 cup fresh spinach, minced

- 1/4 cup feta cheese, crumbled

- 5 large eggs

- Pinch of salt

- Pinch of pepper

- 1 1/2 tbsp Pesto sauce

- Fresh basil for garnish

Directions:

1. Preheat oven to 400 degrees F

2. Spray a muffin tin with cooking spray, generously

3. Line each of the muffin tin with 1 ½ pieces of ham - making sure there aren't any holes for the egg mixture come out of

4. Place some of the roasted red pepper in the bottom of each muffin tin

5. Place 1 tbsp of minced spinach on top of each red pepper

6. Top the pepper and spinach off with a large 1/2 tbsp of crumbled feta cheese

7. In a medium bowl, whisk together the eggs salt and pepper, divide the egg mixture evenly among the 6 muffin tins

8. Bake for 15 to 17 minutes until the eggs are puffy and set

9. Remove each cup from the muffin tin

10. Allow to cool completely

11. Distribute the muffins among the containers, store in the fridge for 2 - 3days or in the freezer for 3 months

12. To Serve: Heat in the microwave for 30 seconds or until heated through. Garnish with 1/4 tsp pesto sauce, additional roasted red pepper slices and fresh basil.

Nutrition Info:Per Serving: Calories:109;Carbs: 2g;Total Fat: 6g;Protein: 9g

Overnight Berry Chia Oats

Servings: 1

Cooking Time: 5 Minutes

Ingredients:

- 1/2 cup Quaker Oats rolled oats

- 1/4 cup chia seeds

- 1 cup milk or water

- pinch of salt and cinnamon

- maple syrup, or a different sweetener, to taste

- 1 cup frozen berries of choice or smoothie leftovers

- Toppings:

- Yogurt

- Berries

Directions:

1. In a jar with a lid, add the oats, seeds, milk, salt, and cinnamon, refrigerate overnight

2. On serving day, puree the berries in a blender

3. Stir the oats, add in the berry puree and top with yogurt and more berries, nuts, honey, or garnish of your choice

4. Enjoy!

5. Recipe Notes: Make 3 jars at a time in individual jars for easy grab and go breakfasts for the next few days.

Nutrition Info:Per Serving: Calories:405;Carbs: g;Total Fat: 11g;Protein: 17g

Quinoa

Servings: 4

Cooking Time: 8 Hours

Ingredients:

- 1 cup quinoa (uncooked)

- 2 cups water

- 1 tablespoon raw honey

- 1 cup coconut milk

- Topping(s) of your preference (nuts, cinnamon, etc.)

- sea salt or plain salt

Directions:

1. Start by rinsing the quinoa under running water.

2. Then, add all the Ingredients: in a slow cooker and cover with a lid. Cook the mixture for 8 hours on low.

3. Serve hot with toppings of your choice.

Nutrition Info:Per Serving: Calories: 310, Total Fat: 16.8g, Saturated Fat: 13, Cholesterol: 0 mg, Sodium: 11 mg, Total Carbohydrate: 39 g, Dietary Fiber: 4.3 g, Total Sugars: 6.3 g, Protein: 7.4 g, Vitamin D: 0 mcg, Calcium: 30 mg, Iron: 3 mg, Potassium: 400 mg

Egg, Feta, Spinach, And Artichoke Freezer Breakfast Burritos

Servings: 6

Cooking Time: 5 Minutes

Ingredients:

- 8 large eggs

- ½ teaspoon dried Italian herbs

- ½ teaspoon garlic powder

- ½ teaspoon onion powder

- 3 teaspoons olive oil, divided

- 10 ounces baby spinach leaves

- ½ cup crumbled feta cheese

- 1 (14-ounce) can quartered artichoke hearts, super-tough leaves removed

- 6 (8- or 9-inch) whole-wheat tortillas

- 6 tablespoons prepared hummus or homemade hummus

Directions:

1. Beat the eggs and whisk in the Italian herbs, garlic powder, and onion powder.

2. Heat 1 teaspoon of oil in a 1inch skillet. When the oil is shimmering, add the spinach and sauté for 2 to 3 minutes, until the spinach is wilted. Remove the spinach from the pan.

3. In the same pan, heat the remaining 2 teaspoons of oil. When the oil is hot, add the eggs. When the eggs start to set, stir to scramble. Cook for about minutes, then add the cooked spinach, feta, and artichoke hearts. Cool the mixture and pour off any liquid if it accumulates.

4. Place 1 tortilla on a cutting board. Spread 1 tablespoon of hummus down the middle of the

tortilla. Place ¾ cup of the egg filling on top of the hummus. Fold the bottom end and sides over the filling and tightly roll up. Repeat for the remaining 5 tortillas.

5. Wrap each burrito in foil and place in a resealable plastic bag.

6. STORAGE: Store sealed bags in the freezer for up to 3 months. To reheat burritos, unwrap and remove the foil. Cover the burrito with a damp paper towel, place on a microwaveable plate, and microwave on high until the center of the burrito is hot, about 2 minutes.

Nutrition Info:Per Serving: Total calories: 359; Total fat: 18g; Saturated fat: 6g; Sodium: 800mg; Carbohydrates: 32g; Fiber: 6g; Protein: 18g

Breakfast Jalapeno Egg Cups

Servings: 6

Cooking Time: 8 Minutes

Ingredients:

- 12 eggs, lightly beaten

- 1/4 tsp garlic powder

- 1/2 tsp lemon pepper seasoning

- 3 jalapeno peppers, chopped

71

- 1 cup cheddar cheese, shredded

- Pepper

- Salt

Directions:

1. Pour 1/2 cups of water into the instant pot then place steamer rack in the pot.

2. In a bowl, whisk eggs with lemon pepper seasoning, garlic powder, pepper, and salt.

3. Stir in jalapenos and cheese.

4. Pour mixture between six jars and seal jar with a lid.

5. Place jars on top of the rack in the instant pot.

6. Seal pot with a lid and select manual and set timer for 8 minutes.

7. Once done, allow to release pressure naturally for 10 minutes then release remaining using quick release. Remove lid.

8. Serve and enjoy.

Nutrition Info: Calories: 212;Fat: 15.2 g;Carbohydrates: 3.2 g;Sugar: 2.1 g;Protein: 16.1 g;Cholesterol: 347 mg

Low Carb Waffles

Servings: 2

Cooking Time: 10 Minutes

Ingredients:

- 4 egg whites

- 2 whole eggs

- ½ teaspoon baking powder

- 4 tablespoons milk

- 4 tablespoons coconut flour

- sugar or sweetener to taste

Directions:

1. Whip the egg whites to a stiff peak.

2. When the stiff peaks are attained, add the coconut flour, milk, baking powder, and the whole egg; mix.

3. Start heating your waffle iron to the required temperature. Grease it and pour in the batter. Cook until brown.

4. Serve warm and top with your choice of fruit or other toppings.

Nutrition Info:Per Serving: Calories: 234, Total Fat: 9.1g, Saturated Fat: 7, Cholesterol: 166 mg, Sodium: 204 mg, Total Carbohydrate: 18.9 g, Dietary Fiber: 10 g, Total Sugars: 4.2 g, Protein: 17.7 g, Vitamin D: 16 mcg, Calcium: 118 mg, Iron: 1 mg, Potassium: 310 mg

Potato Breakfast Hash

Servings: 2

Cooking Time: 10 Minutes

Ingredients:

- 1 sweet potato, diced

- 1 cup bell pepper, chopped

- 1 tsp cumin

- 1 tbsp olive oil

- 1 potato, diced

- 1/2 tsp pepper

- 1 tsp paprika

- 1/2 tsp garlic, minced

- 1/4 cup vegetable stock

- 1/2 tsp salt

Directions:

1. Add all ingredients into the instant pot and stir well.

2. Seal pot with lid and cook on high for 10 minutes.

3. Once done, release pressure using quick release. Remove lid.

4. Stir and serve.

Nutrition Info: Calories: 206;Fat: 7.7 g;Carbohydrates: 32.9 g;Sugar: 7.6 g;Protein: 4 g;Cholesterol: 0 mg

Farro Porridge With Blackberry Compote

Servings: 4

Cooking Time: 30 Minutes

Ingredients:

- 1¼ cups uncooked semi-pearled farro

- 5 cups unsweetened vanilla almond milk

- 1 tablespoon pure maple syrup

- 1 (10-ounce) package frozen blackberries (2 cups)

- 2 teaspoons pure maple syrup

- 2 teaspoons balsamic vinegar

Directions:

1. TO MAKE THE FARRO

2. Place the farro, almond milk, and maple syrup in a saucepan. Bring the liquid to a boil, then turn the heat down to low and simmer until the farro is tender and has absorbed much of the liquid, about 30 minutes. It should still look somewhat liquidy and will continue to absorb liquid as it cools.

3. Scoop ¾ cup of farro into each of 4 containers.

4. TO MAKE THE BLACKBERRY COMPOTE

5. While the farro is cooking, place the frozen blackberries, maple syrup, and balsamic vinegar in a separate saucepan on medium-low heat. Cook for 12 to 1minutes, until the blackberry juices have thickened. Cool.

6. Spoon ¼ cup of the blackberry compote into each of the 4 farro containers.

7. STORAGE: Store covered containers in the refrigerator for up to 5 days.

Nutrition Info:Per Serving: Total calories: 334; Total fat: 5g; Saturated fat: 0g; Sodium: 227mg; Carbohydrates: 64g; Fiber: 11g; Protein: 11g

Bulgur Fruit Breakfast Bowl

Servings: 6

Cooking Time: 15 Minutes

Ingredients:

- 2 cups 2% milk

- ½ teaspoon ground cinnamon

- 1 ½ cups bulgur

- ½ cup almonds, chopped

- ½ cup mint, chopped (fresh is preferred)

- 8 dried and chopped figs

- 1 cup water

- 2 cups frozen sweet cherries - you can also substitute in blueberries or blackberries

Directions:

1. Turn your stovetop to medium heat and combine the bulger, water, milk, and cinnamon. Lightly stir as the ingredients come to a boil.

2. Cover your mixture and turn the stove range temperature down to medium-low heat. Let the mixture simmer for 8 to 11 minutes. It is done simmering when about half of the liquid has been absorbed

3. Without removing the pan, turn off the rangetop heat and add the frozen cherries, almonds, and figs. Lightly stir and then cover for one minute so the cherries can thaw, and the mixture can combine.

4. Remove the cover and add in the mint before scooping your breakfast into a bowl.

Nutrition Info: calories: 301, fats: 6 grams, carbohydrates: grams, protein: 9 grams.

Acorn Squash Eggs

Servings: 5

Cooking Time: 30 Minutes

Ingredients:

- 2 acorn squash

- 4 eggs

- 2 tablespoons extra virgin olive oil

- salt

- pepper

- 5-6 dates, pitted

- 8 walnut halves

- bunch fresh parsley

Directions:

1. Preheat oven to 375 degrees F.

2. Cut the squashes crosswise into ¾-inch thick slices; remove seeds.

3. Prepare slices with holes.

4. Line a baking sheet with parchment paper and place the slices on it.

5. Season with salt and pepper and bake for 20 minutes.

6. Chop up walnuts and dates.

7. Remove the baking dish from the oven and drizzle the slices with olive oil.

8. Crack an egg into the center of the slices (into the hole you made) and season with salt and pepper.

9. Sprinkle walnuts on top and put back in the oven for 10 minutes.

10. Add maple syrup.

11. Enjoy!

Nutrition Info:Per Serving: Calories: 198, Total Fat: 9.5g, Saturated Fat: 2, Cholesterol: 131 mg, Sodium: 97 mg, Total Carbohydrate: 25.7 g, Dietary Fiber: 3.9 g, Total Sugars: 5.7 g, Protein: 6.6 g, Vitamin D: mcg, Calcium: 107 mg, Iron: 3 mg, Potassium: 811 mg

Green Smoothie

Servings: 2

Cooking Time: 12 Minutes

Ingredients:

- 4 cups spinach

- 20 almonds, raw

- 2 cups milk

- 2 scoops whey protein

- sweetener of your choice and to taste

Directions:

1. Start by blending spinach, almond, and milk in a blender.

2. Blend until the puree is formed.

3. Add the rest of the Ingredients: and blend well.

4. Pour into glasses and serve.

5. Enjoy.

Nutrition Info:Per Serving: Calories: 325, Total Fat: 13.1 g, Saturated Fat: 4.4 g, Cholesterol: 85 mg, Sodium: 218 mg, Total Carbohydrate: 20.4 g, Dietary Fiber: 2.8 g, Total Sugars: 12.7 g, Protein: 34.4 g, Vitamin D: 1 mcg, Calcium: 482 mg, Iron: 3 mg, Potassium: 738 mg

Thick Pomegranate Cherry Smoothie

Servings: 4

Cooking Time: 5 Minutes

Ingredients:

- 16 ounces frozen dark cherries

- ¾ cup pomegranate juice

- 1 teaspoon vanilla extract

- 6 ice cubes

- ½ cup pomegranate seeds

- 1 ½ cups Greek yogurt, plain

- ⅓ cup milk

- ¾ teaspoon ground cinnamon

- ½ cup pistachios, chopped

Directions:

1. Add the ice cubes, cherries, pomegranate juice, yogurt, vanilla, milk, and cinnamon into a blender. Mix until the ingredients are smooth. It is thicker than your average smoothie.

2. Instead of a cup, divide the smoothie into four bowls.

3. Sprinkle chopped pistachios and pomegranate seeds on top of the smoothie.

4. Serve and enjoy!

Nutrition Info: calories: 212, fats: 7 grams, carbohydrates: 3grams, protein: 4 grams.

Honey Nut Granola

Servings: 6

Cooking Time: 30 Minutes

Ingredients:

- ¼ cup honey

- 2 ½ cups rolled oats

- ¼ teaspoon sea salt

- 2 tablespoons ground flaxseed

- 2 teaspoons vanilla extract

- ⅓ cup chopped almonds

- ½ teaspoon ground cinnamon

- ¼ cup olive oil

- ½ cup dried apricots, chopped

Directions:

1. Set the temperature of your oven to 325 degrees Fahrenheit and line a baking pan with a piece of parchment paper. While you can grease the pan, it is easier to use parchment paper when you're cutting the granola.

2. Turn a burner on your stovetop to medium heat and add the salt, chopped almonds, cinnamon, and oats. Cook the mixture for 5 to 6 minutes while stirring occasionally.

3. Using a microwavable-safe dish, mix the flaxseed, apricots, oil, and honey. Set the mixture in your microwave and the timer for 1 minute. If the mixture does not bubble within the minute, continue for another minute or until the mixture bubbles.

4. Mix the vanilla into the flaxseed mixture and then pour this mixture over the almond and oats mixture. Combine the ingredients thoroughly.

5. Remove the skillet from heat and pour onto the parchment paper. Spread the mixture as evenly as possible with a spatula or another sheet of parchment paper and your hand.

6. Set the pan into the oven and turn your timer to 15 minutes. However, you want to watch the granola closely as once it starts to brown, you'll need to remove it from heat.

7. Set the granola aside to cool thoroughly. If you used parchment paper, you can take the granola out of the pan by holding the paper and

setting it on your counter. It will cool faster so you can eat it faster! Once this waiting is done, cut or break apart the granola into small pieces and enjoy!

Nutrition Info: calories: 337, fats: 17 grams, carbohydrates: 42 grams, protein: 7 grams.

Quinoa Granola

Servings: 2

Cooking Time: 25 Minutes

Ingredients:

- 1 cup Old-Fashioned rolled oats, or gluten-free

- 1/2 cup uncooked white quinoa

- 2 cups raw almonds, roughly chopped

- 1 Tbsp coconut sugar or sub organic brown sugar, muscovado, or organic cane sugar

- 1 pinch sea salt

- 3 1/2 tbsp coconut oil

- 1/4 cup maple syrup or agave nectar

Directions:

1. Preheat oven to 340 degrees F

2. In a large mixing bowl, add the quinoa, almonds, oats, coconut sugar, and salt, stir to combine

3. To a small saucepan, add the maple syrup and coconut oil, warm over medium heat for 2-minutes, whisking frequently until completely mixed and combined

4. Immediately pour over the dry ingredients, stir to combine and thoroughly all oats and nuts

5. Arrange on a large baking sheet, spread into an even layer

6. Bake for 20 minutes

7. Then remove from oven, stir and toss the granola - make sure to turn the pan around so the other end goes into the oven first and bakes

8. evenly

9. Bake for 5-10 minutes more - watch carefully so it doesn't burn and it's golden brown and very fragrant

10. Allow to cool completely, then store in a container for up to 7 days

Nutrition Info:Per Serving: Calories:332;Total Carbohydrates: 30g;Total Fat: 20g;Protein: 9g

Greek Yogurt With Fresh Berries, Honey And Nuts

Servings: 1

Cooking Time: 5 Minutes

Ingredients:

- 6 oz. nonfat plain Greek yogurt

- 1/2 cup fresh berries of your choice

- 1 tbsp .25 oz crushed walnuts

- 1 tbsp honey

Directions:

1. In a jar with a lid, add the yogurt

2. Top with berries and a drizzle of honey

3. Top with the lid and store in the fridge for 2-days

4. To Serve: Add the granola or nuts, enjoy

Nutrition   Info:Per   Serving: Calories:2;Carbs: 35g;Total Fat: 4g;Protein: 19g

Quinoa Bake With Banana

Servings: 8

Cooking Time: 1 Hour 20 Minutes

Ingredients:

- 3 cups medium over-ripe Bananas, mashed

- 1/4 cup molasses

- 1/4 cup pure maple syrup

- 1 tbsp cinnamon

- 2 tsp raw vanilla extract

- 1 tsp ground ginger

- 1 tsp ground cloves

- 1/2 tsp ground allspice

- 1/2 tsp salt

- 1 cup quinoa, uncooked

- 2 1/2 cups unsweetened vanilla almond milk

- 1/4 cup slivered almonds

Directions:

1. In the bottom of a 2 2-3-quart casserole dish, mix together the mashed banana, maple syrup, cinnamon, vanilla extract, ginger, cloves, allspice, molasses, and salt until well mixed

2. Add in the quinoa, stir until the quinoa is evenly in the banana mixture.

3. Whisk in the almond milk, mix until well combined, cover and refrigerate overnight or bake immediately

4. Heat oven to 350 degrees F

5. Whisk the quinoa mixture making sure it doesn't settle to the bottom

6. Cover the pan with tinfoil and bake until the liquid is absorbed, and the top of the quinoa is set, about 1 hour to 1 hour and 15 mins

7. Turn the oven to high broil, uncover the pan, sprinkle with sliced almonds, and lightly press them into the quinoa

8. Broil until the almonds just turn golden brown, about 2-4 minutes, watching closely, as they burn quickly

9. Allow to cool for 10 minutes then slice the quinoa bake

10. Distribute the quinoa bake among the containers, store in the fridge for 3-4 days

Nutrition Info:Per Serving: Calories:213;Carbs: 41g;Total Fat: 4g;Protein: 5g

Pear And Mango Smoothie

Servings: 1

Cooking Time: 10 Minutes

Ingredients:

- ½ peeled, pitted, and chopped mango

- 2 cubes of ice

- 1 ripe, cored, and chopped pear

- ½ cup of plain Greek yogurt

- 1 cup chopped kale

Directions:

1. In a blender, combine the mango, ice cubes, pear, yogurt, and kale.

2. Blend until the mixture is smooth and thick.

3. Serve and enjoy!

Nutrition Info: calories: 293, fats: 8 grams, carbohydrates: 53 grams, protein: 8 grams.

Cappuccino Muffins

Servings: 2

Cooking Time: 20 Minutes

Ingredients:

- 2 1/3 cups all-purpose flour

- 2 tsp baking powder

- 1 tsp salt

- 1 tsp ground cinnamon

- ¾ cup hot water

- 2 tbsp espresso powder or instant coffee

- 2 eggs

- 1 cup sugar

- ¾ cup vegetable oil

- 1/3 cup mini chocolate chips

- ¼ cup milk

Directions:

1. Preheat oven to 425 degree F

2. In a medium bowl, whisk together the flour, baking powder, salt and cinnamon, set aside

3. In a small bowl, combine the hot water and espresso powder, stir to dissolve, add milk, stir to combine and set aside

4. In a large bowl, whisk together eggs, sugar and oil, slowly add the coffee mixture, and stir to combine Then add in the dry ingredients in thirds, whisking gently until smooth

5. Add in the chocolate chips, stir to combine

6. Place the muffin papers in a 12-cup muffin tin

7. Fill each cup half way

8. Bake for 17-20 minutes, until risen and set

9. Allow to cool completely before slicing

10. Wrap the slices in plastic wrap and then aluminum foil and store in fridge for up to 4-5 days

11. To Serve: Remove the aluminum foil and plastic wrap, and microwave for 2 minutes, then allow to rest for 30 seconds, enjoy!

Nutrition Info:Per Serving:(1 muffin): Calories:201;Carbs: 29g;Total Fat: 8g;Protein: 2g

Feta Spinach Egg Cups

Servings: 4

Cooking Time: 8 Minutes

Ingredients:

- 6 eggs

- 1/4 tsp garlic powder

- 1 tomato, chopped

- 1/4 cup feta cheese, crumbled

- 1 cup spinach, chopped

- 1/2 cup mozzarella cheese, shredded

- Pepper

- salt

Directions:

1. Pour 1/2 cups of water into the instant pot then place steamer rack in the pot.

2. In a bowl, whisk eggs with garlic powder, pepper, and salt.

3. Add remaining ingredients and stir well.

4. Spray four ramekins with cooking spray.

5. Pour egg mixture into the ramekins and place ramekins on top of the rack.

6. Seal pot with lid and cook on high for 8 minutes.

7. Once done, release pressure using quick release. Remove lid.

8. Serve and enjoy.

Nutrition Info: Calories: 134;Fat: 3 g;Carbohydrates: 2 g;Sugar: 1.4 g;Protein: 11 g;Cholesterol: 256 mg

Chocolate Almond Butter Dip

Servings: 5

Cooking Time: 10 Minutes

Ingredients:

- 1 cup of Plain Greek Yogurt

- ½ cup almond butter

- 1/3 cup chocolate hazelnut spread

- 1 tablespoon honey

- 1 teaspoon vanilla

- sliced up fruits as you desire, such as pears, apples, apricots, bananas, etc.

Directions:

1. Take a medium-sized bowl and add all Ingredients: except the fruit.

2. Take an immersion blender and blend everything well until a smooth dip forms.

3. Alternatively, you can Directions:the Ingredients: in a food processor as well.

4. Serve with your favorite fruit slices!

Nutrition Info:Per Serving: Calories: 148, Total Fat: 7.3 g, Saturated Fat: 1.8 g, Cholesterol: 1 mg, Sodium: 26 mg, Total Carbohydrate: 17 g, Dietary Fiber: 0.7 g, Total Sugars: 15 g, Protein: 5.9 g, Vitamin D: 0 mcg, Calcium: 37 mg, Iron: 0 mg, Potassium: 15 mg

Sun Dried Tomatoes, Dill And Feta Omelette Casserole

Servings: 6

Cooking Time: 40

Ingredients:

- 12 large eggs

- 2 cups whole milk

- 8 oz fresh spinach

- 2 cloves garlic, minced

- 12 oz artichoke salad with olives and peppers, drained and chopped

- 5 oz sun dried tomato feta cheese, crumbled

- 1 tbsp fresh chopped dill or 1 tsp dried dill

- 1 tsp dried oregano

- 1 tsp lemon pepper

- 1 tsp salt

- 4 tsp olive oil, divided

Directions:

1. Preheat oven to 375 degrees F

2. Chop the fresh herbs and artichoke salad

3. In a skillet over medium heat, add 1 tbsp olive oil

4. Sauté the spinach and garlic until wilted, about 3 minutes

5. Oil a 9x13 inch baking dish, layer the spinach and artichoke salad evenly in the dish

6. In a medium bowl, whisk together the eggs, milk, herbs, salt and lemon pepper

7. Pour the egg mixture over vegetables, sprinkle with feta cheese

8. Bake in the center of the oven for 35-40 minutes until firm in the center

9. Allow to cool, slice a and distribute among the storage containers. Store for 2-3 days or freeze for 3 months

10. To Serve: Reheat in the microwave for 30 seconds or until heated through or in the toaster oven for 5 minutes or until heated through

Nutrition Info:Per Serving: Calories:196;Total Carbohydrates: 5g;Total Fat: 12g;Protein: 10g

Desserts Recipes

Cherry Brownies With Walnuts

Servings: 9

Cooking Time: 25 To 30 Minutes

Ingredients:

- 9 fresh cherries that are stemmed and pitted or 9 frozen cherries

- ½ cup sugar or sweetener substitute

- ¼ cup extra virgin olive oil

- 1 teaspoon vanilla extract

- ¼ teaspoon sea salt

- ½ cup whole-wheat pastry flour

- ¼ teaspoon baking powder

- ⅓ cup walnuts, chopped

- 2 eggs

- ½ cup plain Greek yogurt

- ⅓ cup cocoa powder, unsweetened

Directions:

1. Make sure one of the metal racks in your oven is set in the middle.

2. Turn the temperature on your oven to 375 degrees Fahrenheit.

3. Using cooking spray, grease a 9-inch square pan.

4. Take a large bowl and add the oil and sugar or sweetener substitute. Whisk the ingredients well.

5. Add the eggs and use a mixer to beat the ingredients together.

6. Pour in the yogurt and continue to beat the mixture until it is smooth.

7. Take a medium bowl and combine the cocoa powder, flour, sea salt, and baking powder by whisking them together.

8. Combine the powdered ingredients into the wet ingredients and use your electronic mixer to incorporate the ingredients together thoroughly.

9. Add in the walnuts and stir.

10. Pour the mixture into the pan.

11. Sprinkle the cherries on top and push them into the batter. You can use any design, but it is best to make three rows and three columns with the cherries. This ensures that each piece of the brownie will have one cherry.

12. Put the batter into the oven and turn your timer to 20 minutes.

13. Check that the brownies are done using the toothpick test before removing them from the oven. Push the toothpick into the middle of the brownies and once it comes out clean, remove the brownies.

14. Let the brownies cool for 5 to 10 minutes before cutting and serving.

Nutrition Info: calories: 225, fats: 10 grams, carbohydrates: 30 grams, protein: 5 grams.

Fruit Dip

Servings: 10

Cooking Time: 10 To 15 Minutes

Ingredients:

- ¼ cup coconut milk, full-fat is best

- ¼ cup vanilla yogurt

- ⅓ cup marshmallow creme

- 1 cup cream cheese, set at room temperature

- 2 tablespoons maraschino cherry juice

Directions:

1. In a large bowl, add the coconut milk, vanilla yogurt, marshmallow creme, cream cheese, and cherry juice.

2. Using an electric mixer, set to low speed and blend the ingredients together until the fruit dip is smooth.

3. Serve the dip with some of your favorite fruits and enjoy!

Nutrition Info: calories: 110, fats: 11 grams, carbohydrates: 3 grams, protein: 3 grams.

A Lemony Treat

Servings: 4

Cooking Time: 30 Minutes

Ingredients:

- 1 lemon, medium in size

- 1 ½ teaspoons cornstarch

- 1 cup Greek yogurt, plain is best

- Fresh fruit

- ¼ cup cold water

- ⅔ cup heavy whipped cream

- 3 tablespoons honey

- Optional: mint leaves

Directions:

1. Take a large glass bowl and your metal, electric mixer and set them in the refrigerator so they can chill.

2. In a separate bowl, add the yogurt and set that in the fridge.

3. Zest the lemon into a medium bowl that is microwavable.

4. Cut the lemon in half and then squeeze 1 tablespoon of lemon juice into the bowl.

5. Combine the cornstarch and water. Mix the ingredients thoroughly.

6. Pour in the honey and whisk the ingredients together.

7. Put the mixture into the microwave for 1 minute on high.

8. Once the microwave stops, remove the mixture and stir.

9. Set it back into the microwave for 15 to 30 seconds or until the mixture starts to bubble and thicken.

10. Take the bowl of yogurt from the fridge and pour in the warm mixture while whisking.

11. Put the yogurt mixture back into the fridge.

12. Take the large bowl and beaters out of the fridge.

13. Put your electronic mixer together and pour the whipped cream into the chilled bowl.

14. Beat the cream until soft peaks start to form. This can take up to 3 minutes, depending on how fresh your cream is.

15. Remove the yogurt from the fridge.

16. Fold the yogurt into the cream using a rubber spatula. Remember to lift and turn the mixture so it doesn't deflate.

17. Place back into the fridge until you are serving the dessert or for 15 minutes. The dessert should not be in the fridge for longer than 1 hour.

18. When you serve the lemony goodness, you will spoon it into four dessert dishes and drizzle with extra honey or even melt some chocolate to drizzle on top.

19. Add a little fresh mint and enjoy!

Nutrition Info: calories: 241, fats: 16 grams, carbohydrates: 21 grams, protein: 7 grams.

Melon With Ginger

Servings: 4

Cooking Time: 10 To 15 Minutes

Ingredients:

- ½ cantaloupe, cut into 1-inch chunks

- 2 cups of watermelon, cut into 1-inch chunks

- 2 cups honeydew melon, cut into 1-inch chunks

- 2 tablespoons of raw honey

- Ginger, 2 inches in size, peeled, grated, and preserve the juice

Directions:

1. In a large bowl, combine your cantaloupe, honeydew melon, and watermelon. Gently mix the ingredients.

2. Combine the ginger juice and stir.

3. Drizzle on the honey, serve, and enjoy! You can also chill the mixture for up to an hour before serving.

Nutrition Info: calories: 91, fats: 0 grams, carbohydrates: 23 grams, protein: 1 gram.

Almond Shortbread Cookies

Servings: 16

Cooking Time: 25 Minutes

Ingredients:

- ½ cup coconut oil

- 1 teaspoon vanilla extract

- 2 egg yolks

- 1 tablespoon brandy

- 1 cup powdered sugar

- 1 cup finely ground almonds

- 3 ½ cups cake flour

- ½ cup almond butter

- 1 tablespoon water or rose flower water

Directions:

1. In a large bowl, combine the coconut oil, powdered sugar, and butter. If the butter is not soft, you want to wait until it softens up. Use an electric mixer to beat the ingredients together at high speed.

2. In a small bowl, add the egg yolks, brandy, water, and vanilla extract. Whisk well.

3. Fold the egg yolk mixture into the large bowl.

4. Add the flour and almonds. Fold and mix with a wooden spoon.

5. Place the mixture into the fridge for at least 1 hour and 30 minutes.

6. Preheat your oven to 325 degrees Fahrenheit.

7. Take the mixture, which now looks like dough, and divide it into 1-inch balls.

8. With a piece of parchment paper on a baking sheet, arrange the cookies and flatten them with a fork or your fingers.

9. Place the cookies in the oven for 13 minutes, but watch them so they don't burn.

10. Transfer the cookies onto a rack to cool for a couple of minutes before enjoying!

Nutrition Info: calories: 250, fats: 14 grams, carbohydrates: 30 grams, protein: 3 grams.

Chocolate Fruit Kebabs

Servings: 6

Cooking Time: 30 Minutes

Ingredients:

- 24 blueberries

- 12 strawberries with the green leafy top part removed

- 12 green or red grapes, seedless

- 12 pitted cherries

- 8 ounces chocolate

Directions:

1. Line a baking sheet with a piece of parchment paper and place 6, -inch long wooden skewers on top of the paper.

2. Start by threading a piece of fruit onto the skewers. You can create and follow any pattern that you like with the ingredients. An example pattern is 1 strawberry, 1 cherry, blueberries, 2 grapes. Repeat the pattern until all of the fruit is on the skewers.

3. In a saucepan on medium heat, melt the chocolate. Stir continuously until the chocolate has melted completely.

4. Carefully scoop the chocolate into a plastic sandwich bag and twist the bag closed starting right above the chocolate.

5. Snip the corner of the bag with scissors.

6. Drizzle the chocolate onto the kebabs by squeezing it out of the bag.

7. Put the baking pan into the freezer for 20 minutes.

8. Serve and enjoy!

Nutrition Info: calories: 254, fats: 15 grams, carbohydrates: 28 grams, protein: 4 grams.

Peaches With Blue Cheese Cream

Servings: 4

Cooking Time: 20 Hours 10 Minutes

Ingredients:

- 4 peaches

- 1 cinnamon stick

- 4 ounces sliced blue cheese

- ⅓ cup orange juice, freshly squeezed is best

- 3 whole cloves

- 1 teaspoon of orange zest, taken from the orange peel

- ¼ teaspoon cardamom pods

- ⅔ cup red wine

- 2 tablespoons honey, raw or your preferred variety

- 1 vanilla bean

- 1 teaspoon allspice berries

- 4 tablespoons dried cherries

Directions:

1. Set a saucepan on top of your stove range and add the cinnamon stick, cloves, orange juice, cardamom, vanilla, allspice, red wine, and orange zest. Whisk the ingredients well.

2. Add your peaches to the mixture and poach them for hours or until they become soft.

3. Take a spoon to remove the peaches and boil the rest of the liquid to make the syrup. You want the liquid to reduce itself by at least half.

4. While the liquid is boiling, combine the dried cherries, blue cheese, and honey into a bowl.

5. Once your peaches are cooled, slice them into halves.

6. Top each peach with the blue cheese mixture and then drizzle the liquid onto the top.

7. Serve and enjoy!

Nutrition Info: calories: 211, fats: 24 grams, carbohydrates: 15 grams, protein: 6 grams.

Mediterranean Blackberry Ice Cream

Servings: 6

Cooking Time: 15 Minutes

Ingredients:

- 3 egg yolks

- 1 container of Greek yogurt

- 1 pound mashed blackberries

- ½ teaspoon vanilla essence

- 1 teaspoon arrowroot powder

- ¼ teaspoon ground cloves

- 5 ounces sugar or sweetener substitute

- 1 pound heavy cream

Directions:

1. In a small bowl, add the arrowroot powder and egg yolks. Whisk or beat them with an electronic mixture until they are well combined.

2. Set a saucepan on top of your stove and turn your heat to medium.

3. Add the heavy cream and bring it to a boil.

4. Turn off the heat and add the egg mixture into the cream through folding.

5. Turn the heat back on to medium and pour in the sugar. Cook the mixture for 10 minutes or until it starts to thicken.

6. Remove the mixture from heat and place it in the fridge so it can completely cool. This should take about one hour.

7. Once the mixture is cooled, add in the Greek yogurt, ground cloves, blackberries, and vanilla by folding in the ingredients.

8. Transfer the ice cream into a container and place it in the freezer for at least two hours.

9. Serve and enjoy!

Nutrition Info: calories: 402, fats: 20 grams, carbohydrates: 52 grams, protein: 8 grams.

Stuffed Figs

Servings: 6

Cooking Time: 20 Minutes

Ingredients:

- 10 halved fresh figs

- 20 chopped almonds

- 4 ounces goat cheese, divided

- 2 tablespoons of raw honey

Directions:

1. Turn your oven to broiler mode and set it to a high temperature.

2. Place your figs, cut side up, on a baking sheet. If you like to place a piece of parchment paper on top you can do this, but it is not necessary.

3. Sprinkle each fig with half of the goat cheese.

4. Add a tablespoon of chopped almonds to each fig.

5. Broil the figs for 3 to 4 minutes.

6. Take them out of the oven and let them cool for 5 to 7 minutes.

7. Sprinkle with the remaining goat cheese and honey.

Nutrition Info: calories: 209, fats: 9 grams, carbohydrates: 26 grams, protein: grams.

Chia Pudding With Strawberries

Servings: 4

Cooking Time: 4 Hours 5 Minutes

Ingredients:

- 2 cups unsweetened almond milk

- 1 tablespoon vanilla extract

- 2 tablespoons raw honey

- ¼ cup chia seeds

- 2 cups fresh and sliced strawberries

Directions:

1. In a medium bowl, combine the honey, chia seeds, vanilla, and unsweetened almond milk. Mix well.

2. Set the mixture in the refrigerator for at least 4 hours.

3. When you serve the pudding, top it with strawberries. You can even create a design in a glass serving bowl or dessert dish by adding a little pudding on the bottom, a few strawberries, top the strawberries with some more pudding, and then top the dish with a few strawberries.

Nutrition Info: calories: 108, fats: grams, carbohydrates: 17 grams, protein: 3 grams.

Snacks Recipes

Chunky Monkey Trail Mix

Servings: 6

Cooking Time: 1 Hour 30 Minutes

Ingredients:

- 1 cup cashews, halved

- 2 cups raw walnuts, chopped or halved

- ⅓ cup coconut sugar

- 1 cup coconut flakes, unsweetened and make sure you have big flakes and not shredded

- 6 ounces dried banana slices

- 1 ½ teaspoons coconut oil at room temperature

- 1 teaspoon vanilla extract

- ½ cup of chocolate chips

Directions:

1. Turn your crockpot to high and add the cashews, walnuts, vanilla, coconut oil, and sugar. Combine until the ingredients are well mixed and then cook for 45 minutes.

2. Reduce the temperature on your crockpot to low.

3. Continue to cook the mixture for another 20 minutes.

4. Place a piece of parchment paper on your counter.

5. Once the mix is done cooking, remove it from the crockpot and set on top of the parchment paper.

6. Let the mixture sit and cool for 20 minutes.

7. Pour the contents into a bowl and add the dried bananas and chocolate chips. Gently mix the ingredients together. You can store the mixture in Ziplock bags for a quick and easy snack.

Nutrition Info: calories: 250, fats: 6 grams, carbohydrates: 1grams, protein: 4 grams

Fig-pecan Energy Bites

Servings: 6

Cooking Time: 20 Minutes

Ingredients:

- ½ cup chopped pecans

- 2 tablespoons honey

- ¾ cup dried figs, about 6 to 8, diced

- 2 tablespoons wheat flaxseed

- ¼ cup quick oats

- 2 tablespoons regular or powdered peanut butter

Directions:

1. Combine the figs, quick oats, pecans, peanut butter, and flaxseed into a bowl. Stir the ingredients well.

2. Drizzle honey onto the ingredients and mix everything with a wooden spoon. Do your best to press all the ingredients into the honey as you are stirring. If you start to struggle because the mixture is too sticky, set it in the freezer for 3 to 5 minutes.

3. Divide the mixture into four sections.

4. Take a wet rag and get your hands damp. You don't want them too wet or they won't work well with the mixture.

5. Divide each of the four sections into 3 separate sections.

6. Take one of the three sections and roll them up. Repeat with each section so you have a dozen energy bites once you are done.

7. If you want to firm them up, you can place them into the freezer for a few minutes. Otherwise, you can enjoy them as soon as they are little energy balls.

8. To store them, you'll want to keep them in a sealed container and set them in the fridge. They can be stored for about a week.

Nutrition Info: calories: 157, fats: 6 grams, carbohydrates: 26 grams, protein: 3 grams.

Baked Apples Mediterranean Style

Servings: 4

Cooking Time: 25 Minutes

Ingredients:

- ½ lemon, squeezed for juice

- 1 ½ pounds of peeled and sliced apples

- ¼ teaspoon cinnamon

Directions:

1. Set the temperature of your oven to 350 degrees Fahrenheit so it can preheat.

2. Take a piece of parchment paper and lay on top of a baking pan.

3. Combine your lemon juice, cinnamon, and apples into a medium bowl and mix well.

4. Pour the apples onto the baking pan and arrange them so they are not doubled up.

5. Place the pan in the oven and set your timer to 2minutes. The apples should be tender but not mushy.

6. Remove from the oven, plate and enjoy!

Nutrition Info: calories: 90, fats: 0.3 grams, carbohydrates: 24 grams, protein: 0.5 grams.

Strawberry Popsicle

Servings: 5

Cooking Time: 10 Minutes

Ingredients:

- ½ cup almond milk

- 1 ½ cups fresh strawberries

Directions:

153

1. Using a blender or hand mixer, combine the almond milk and strawberries thoroughly in a bowl.

2. Using popsicle molds, pour the mixture into the molds and place the sticks into the mixture.

3. Set in the freezer for at least 4 hours.

4. Serve and enjoy—especially on a hot day!

5. Nutritional information: calories: 3 fats: 0.5 grams, carbohydrates: 7 grams, protein: 0.6 grams.

Frozen Blueberry Yogurt

Servings: 6

Cooking Time: 30 Minutes

Ingredients:

- ⅔ cup honey

- 2 cups chilled yogurt

- 1 pint fresh blueberries

- 1 juiced and zested lime or lemon. You can even substitute an orange if your tastes prefer.

Directions:

1. With a saucepan on your burner set to medium heat, add the honey, juiced fruit, zest, and blueberries.

2. Stir the mixture continuously as it begins to simmer for 15 minutes.

3. When the liquid is nearly gone, pour the contents into a bowl and place in the fridge for several minutes. You will want to stir the ingredients and check to see if they are chilled.

4. Once the fruit is chilled, combine with the yogurt.

5. Mix until the ingredients are well incorporated and enjoy.

Nutrition Info: calories: 233, fats: 3 grams, carbohydrates: 52 grams, protein: 3.5 grams.

Conclusion

The day and the book is over. But just start making these amazing breakfasts again and you'll start out grittier than ever.

Did you enjoy them? Did you enjoy these recipes to the fullest?

I hope you made them for the whole family, the best time to start the day all together.

Thank you for reading, and get lots of practice making them.

Hugs and thanks

CPSIA information can be obtained
at www.ICGtesting.com
Printed in the USA
BVHW060120250321
603350BV00006B/259